Unraveling Cultural Mysteries

A Guide to Understanding Other Worlds

Table of Contents

Culture is the widening of the mind and of the spirit.

Chapter 1. Introduction

Embark on an extraordinary journey as you dive into "Unraveling Cultural Mysteries: A Guide to Understanding Other Worlds"! This Special Report is your gateway to grasping the intriguing complexities and beauties of various cultures across our diverse planet. From the subtle nuances of social etiquette to in-depth explorations of historical epics - our specially designed guide is all set to whisk you off to an educational adventure. Prepare to be ignited with a newfound excitement for expanding boundaries and deepening understanding, because this isn't just a reading experience, it's a cultural enlightenment! Ready to traverse the landscapes of incredible customs and traditions? Grab your copy today and commence the exploration of a lifetime!

Chapter 2. Mapping the Cultural Terrain: Basic Elements of Culture

There is an intricate tapestry of unique elements that constitute every culture, an array of dimensions that add complexity and richness to the lives of individuals who partake in it. In order to fully grasp the scope and profundity of cultural diversity, it is first essential to understand what comprises these 'Basic Elements of Culture'. What could be more fundamental to understanding culture than learning about its core constituents?

2.1. The Collective Spirit: Societal Norms and Values

Societal norms and values are vital underpinnings within the structural core of culture. Norms define the kind of behavior expected from individuals in a given society, they serve as unstated rules and regulations for acceptable conduct, allowing for cohesion and harmony within a group. Conversely, societal values are beliefs and philosophies that are upheld by a society, often embodying the moral fabric and ideological stances that society maintains.

Understanding societal norms and values is akin to comprehending the unique personality of a society. This collective spirit offers a profound understanding of why societies function the way they do, how they solve disputes, interact with each other, and most importantly, it provides insights into their collective aspirations and fears.

2.2. Symbolism and Rituals: The Unspoken Cultural Threads

Symbols and rituals are non-verbal elements of culture, packed with meaning that those inside the culture can interpret. Rituals, whether they're daily routines or special ceremonies, contribute significantly to the way a society structures their time, relationships, and worldview. These acts, adorned with symbols, can often feel mysterious or even misinterpreted by those outside the culture.

Symbols can take form in various ways including language, clothing, or even common shared experiences. These cultural artifacts have the power to invoke a wealth of emotions and memories in those who are familiar with their intricate meanings. Oftentimes, one symbol or ritual can encapsulate entire stories or historical epochs, making these cultural elements particularly fascinating to explore.

2.3. The Power of Language: Communicating Cultural Identity

Language is a human invention of phenomenal complexity that not only facilitates communication but also carries an intrinsic cultural identity. It is a key element in expressing our thoughts, emotions, desires, and ideas, serving as a bridge connecting people within a particular culture.

The structure of languages, their grammar, syntax, idioms, and even their sounds, indicate numerous aspects about the cultural psychology of a specific community. Understanding a society's language is akin to gaining a backstage pass into their thought process, their world view, and gaining a deeper perception into their historical, social, and cultural contexts.

2.4. Art: The Quintessential Cultural Manifesto

Art is a manifestation of a culture's unique perspectives, a testament to its historical lineage and its contemporary outlook. It helps in conveying cultural values, collective experiences, social phenomenon, spiritual beliefs, and emotional depth of a society. Each cultural artifact, whether it a painting, a sculpture, literature or music, is a narrative that often uses the grammar of symbolism and metaphor to express itself. It becomes a lens through which one can understand the sensibility of a culture and its unique representation of reality.

In conclusion, these basic elements present an overture to the fascinating orchestra that is culture. Yet, this introduction to societal norms and values, symbolism and rituals, language, and art only begins to scratch the surface. As we delve deeper into each individual kingdom of cultural mysteries in the following chapters, we shall unlock a world of understanding previously unimagined. These elements are not isolated entities, but rather a harmonic assembly that when played together, create the symphony of culture. Every thread in the cultural fabric intermingles with another, creating an enchanting tapestry filled with stories and meanings that invite curiosity, reverence, and awe.

Chapter 3. The Thread of Time: Tracing Cultural Evolution

In our monumental journey of cultural exploration, one element that demands our attention is the progression of culture over periods of time. Like a silken thread spinning through an intricate tapestry, the evolution of cultures forms a crucial framework for understanding the complex phenomena that shape our society today.

3.1. In the Beginning: Early Human Cultures

The earliest human cultures emerged as communities gradually transformed into agrarian societies. The invention of agriculture 10,000 years ago marked the first significant cultural shift. People, who had previously survived merely by hunting and gathering, now began to domesticate animals and cultivate plants. Technologies like pottery and metallurgy were born out of the need to store and prepare food, leading to an explosive evolution of inventiveness and creativity.

The role of religion also dates back to this era. As humans grappled with phenomena they couldn't explain, mythologies and deities emerged to comfort them, arguably becoming one of the first forms of cultural evolution. These early societies were structured around primitive religious and social principles which formed the groundwork of civilizations to come.

3.2. Emerging Civilisations: Cultural Revolutions

As the wheel of time turned, the Agricultural Revolution gave way to large, complex civilizations in regions such as Mesopotamia, Egypt, Indus Valley, and China. Each civilization developed distinct structures of governance, religion, art, and technology shaped by their geographical and environmental conditions. This period bore witness to some of the first written languages, legal codes, monumental architecture, and their strong influence continues to ripple through our cultural waters even today.

Cultures began to interact, trade, and, occasionally, conflict with each other, which provided ample ground for cultural borrowing and evolution. One can see fascinating similarities in art, mythology, and social structures across civilizations that had contact with each other, highlighting the fluid nature that culture adopts as it evolves.

3.3. Middle Ages and Renaissance: A Shift in Perspective

The dominantly agrarian society of the Middle Ages saw cultural practices rooted in feudalism, chivalry, and the church. With the dawn of the Renaissance, various cultural transformations unfolded in Europe. An explosion of new ideas in science, exploration, business, religion, and art challenged the established norms.

The Renaissance served as the conduit between the Middle Ages and modern history. It was a period of great cultural change and achievement, marked by renewed interest in ancient Greek and Roman art and philosophies, the development of humanist thinking, and the innovations in science and exploration. This period served not only as the bedrock for the modern Western worldview but also helped broaden understanding of the world beyond the Eurocentric lens.

3.4. Industrial and Digital Age: Era of Rapid Cultural Shifts

The Industrial Revolution fundamentally transformed the societal structure once again. Agrarian societies rapidly morphed into industrialized ones, with people migrating from rural communities to emergent towns and cities. This shift gave rise to a plethora of new cultural practices marked by the common man's fight for political power, the growth of a consumer society, and the dawn of mass communication.

Enter the Digital Age, and we witness culture evolving at an unprecedented speed. Fueled by technological advancements across all fields—communication, information, transport—interactions among diverse cultures have escalated, leading to what anthropologists term 'cultural globalization'. This has blurred traditional cultural boundaries, and in its wake left a myriad of pressing questions about cultural preservation, diversity, and unity.

Throughout the chapters of human history, from the dawn of man to the digital age of today, culture has been ever-evolving. Deeply influenced by changing environments, the innovative spirit of the human race, and interactions with diverse cultures, the ebb and flow of cultural shifts capture the indomitable saga of our collective journey.

In the following sections, we delve into details unfolding intricate facets of language, art, social rituals, music, culinary practices, religion, architecture, and celebrations that form the rich cultural tapestry of our shared human experience. Each insight will bring us closer to understanding the undercurrents of cultural metamorphosis and the remarkable diversity we witness today.

It is only through tracing this thread of time, that we can truly begin to unravel the mysteries embedded in our cultural DNAs, enabling a more inclusive, empathic, and united global community.

Chapter 4. The Language Labyrinth: Unlocking Linguistic Secrets

The intricate latticework of language is indeed a labyrinth for those who venture into it for the first time, with its winding pathways of phonetics, grammar and lexicon. As you begin to explore it, you'll quickly realize that language isn't merely a means of communication, but a complex system that narrates a people's journey through time, whilst revealing the nature and nuances of their civilization and culture.

4.1. The Genesis of Language: Unraveling the Origin Tapestry

Every language that exists, whether spoken by millions or by a few hundred, started somewhere. The story of language evolution is as rich and varied as human history itself, with each turning point leaving its imprint on the lexicon, syntax, and phonetics. Ancient settlers from the earliest of human tribes, to the colossal empires of old cataloged their reality via language, and as territories expanded, or were conquered and then cultivated, languages developed, diverged and converged, creating a fascinating web of lingual kinship and diversity. As you traverse this chapter, you'll witness how languages have dynamically metamorphosed over the millennia, keeping pace with human evolution and cultural shifts whilst retaining unique relics of the past within their phonemic folds.

4.2. Sounds of Significance: Phonetics and Phonology

Sound is the fundamental building block of any spoken language, differing considerably across geographical boundaries. The thorny path of phonetics and phonology takes us through this enchanting world of sound, the study of which is instrumental in understanding both the physiological and acoustic aspects of speech sounds, and their function within specific languages. Elucidating concepts such as consonants, vowels, tone, and stress, this section will provide an analytical lens through which to examine the complexities of sound in communication.

4.3. Story Behind Syntax: Formulating Phrases and Sentences

Moving deeper into the labyrinth, we encounter the walls of syntax. Syntax is the set of rules, principles, and processes dictated by any specific language to structure its sentences. It helps string words together into logical and meaningful phrases, abiding by grammatical rules that, although may feel rigid, have evolved alongside human societies. It lends a fascinating depth to our understanding of structural elements of language, be it word order, agreement, or case marking, unfolding the cultural preferences and practices hidden therein.

4.4. The Lexicon Vault: Words and Meanings

Inside the language labyrinth lies an impenetrable vault that holds thousands, sometimes millions, of semantic elements – the lexicon. Words and their myriad meanings, shaped by the foothills of societal evolution and the rivers of cultural exchange, are set down in this vast repository. Herein we will unearth the art of word creation, spanning from lexical borrowing to the formation of neologisms, each word bearing an etymological tale that hints at deeper socio-historical significance.

4.5. Grammar and Morphology: The Building Blocks

Situated at the heart of the labyrinth are the pillars of grammar and morphology. Studying the ways in which words alter and combine to convey nuances of meaning, reveals how languages differentiate between the real, the hypothetical, the past, the future, the concrete and the abstract, thus highlighting facets of human cognition. By peering through this morphological microscope, we gain insights into the cognitive tools that different cultures have employed to interpret and articulate their world.

4.6. The Hidden Language of Body: Unveiling Non-verbal Communication

Finally, our exploration delves into the non-verbal spectrum of communication. Body language, facial expressions and gestures, those silent forms of communication that whisper volumes on their own, haven't evaded scholarly attention. This section decodes these often overlooked dimensions of cultural linguistics. In understanding these silent dialects, we can gauge a society's unspoken norms, manners, and behavioral cues.

Unraveling language, we discover not simply a mode of interaction, but a complex, dynamic tapestry woven over thousands of years. The labyrinth's twists and turns may prove intimidating at first glance, but they promise the discovery of linguistic secrets, holding a mirror to our cultural identities and histories. This exploration equips us with an enriched understanding; every language leaves a distinct fingerprint on its speakers, a unique pattern that is as instructive as it is captivating.

Chapter 5. Expressions Unveiled: Decoding Art and Symbolism

We commence our exploration into the realm of art and symbolism, which often serve as the most profound representations of a culture's historical narratives, belief systems, and aesthetic sensibilities.

5.1. Exploring the Essence of Art

Art, in its myriad forms, is a ubiquitous human phenomenon that signifies our innate desire to express and communicate. It's a complex interplay of emotions, experiences, ideas, and traditions that build an intricate tapestry of shared cultural expressions. Art essentially is widespread in all cultures, a testament to its deep-rooted human proclivity. From cave paintings scribbled by the dawn of humankind to the grandeur of modern art installations, mankind's journey has been etched in its artistic creations across time and space.

5.2. Cultural Symbols and Their Meanings

Symbols serve as powerful tools to convey a multitude of meanings, often complex and multifaceted, intricately tied to the identity of a culture. A single symbol might represent myriad connotations depending upon the cultural context it is based in. For instance, 'Dragon' symbolizes wisdom and power in Chinese culture while, in Western cultures, it may be associated with evil. Thus, understanding the symbolic language becomes a captivating journey in unravelling the coded wisdom of civilizations.

5.3. Art and Symbolism: From Prehistoric Times to the Modern Age

Art and symbolism hold an inseparable bond, a testimony to how societies use symbols to communicate within their cultural locale.

Petroglyphs, cave drawings, pottery, and other ancient relics from prehistoric times typically depict recognizable symbols such as animals and human figures. Yet, the potential meanings behind them are buried in the ages, challenging us to replay the scenes of an era long past.

As we move forward in time to ancient civilizations, like those of Egypt, Greece, Rome, India, and China, we find symbol-rich narratives in their grand architectures, sculptures, and paintings. These symbols often relate to their cosmology, mythology, and the social order, providing us with an intricate understanding of these civilizations.

The modern age presented a dramatic shift in artistic expressions. Instead of religion and myth-dominated themes, art took a more subjective turn symbolizing thoughts, emotions, and abstract concepts, reflective of the broader societal shifts.

5.4. Decoding the Language of Symbols

Symbols hold great significance in cultural expressions, and deciphering them forms an integral component of this guide. Such decoding enables us to pry open the deeper layers of cultures and grasp the essential nature of their being.

Understanding the context is the first step in decoding the symbolic language. As we've discussed, the same symbol can signify different meanings in different cultures. Therefore, a comprehensive understanding of the socio-cultural context becomes important.

A systematic categorization of symbols as per their representation – religious, spiritual, social, political, or creative expression- can simplify the decoding process. Coupled with the knowledge of history, geography and language inherent to the culture, we can begin to understand the intricate symbolism inherent in arts.

5.5. The Translational Power of Art

Art transcends linguistic barriers. It has the extraordinary potential to communicate across cultures, binding us together in an understanding of shared human experiences. Appreciating the art of another culture is a step towards embracing its ethos, opening doors to mutual respect, empathy, and cross-cultural friendships. It's a testament to art's power to reflect and connect us as social beings, narrating tales of our shared history, our divergent paths, and our common hopes.

5.6. Art as a Medium for Cultural Preservation

Art and symbolism, in their myriad forms, provide a treasure trove of cultural information. They serve as a resilient medium to preserve and pass on cultural knowledge and heritage through generations, thereby playing a pivotal role in cultural longevity. Every brush stroke on a canvas, every chisel on a stone, every rhythm in a song, captures and encapsulates a piece of cultural wisdom.

The exploration of the expressive arts of a culture and delving into its symbolic language, is indeed akin to embarking on a fascinating journey through time and space, where every stop is an enlightening encounter with a distinct facet of human creativity and spirit. Be it a mesmerizing melody from an ancient tribe, or an avant-garde painting in a modern art gallery, each artistic creation tells a story sewn into the fabric of its culture, awaiting to be unraveled by those who dare to delve deep. Through this chapter, we hope to have ignited within you, a passion for appreciating and understanding the vibrant tapestry of culture through its expressive arts and intricate symbolism.

Chapter 6. Social Etiquette and Rituals: The Unspoken Language

In the intricate tapestry that forms the human cultural experience, social etiquette and rituals play a fundamental, yet often overlooked, role. They constitute the unspoken language through which communities interact, engage, and communicate their values. Like the threading in a delicate embroidery, these customs weave together to create a living, evolving depiction of what it means to be a part of a particular culture.

6.1. Universality and Variability of Social Etiquette

Worldwide, social etiquette exists in varying forms, reflective of the diverse makeup of cultural landscapes. Yet, there remains a commonality between them – a unifying code permeating through every culture that fosters mutual respect, recognition, and peace. From the intricate bowing rituals in Japan to the warm and vigorously firm handshakes of African tribes, these gestures are evidence of a common human endeavor – the desire to convey respect, goodwill and peaceful interaction.

The variability in this etiquette becomes evidently clear when studied from a regional perspective. For instance, while maintaining eye contact is viewed as confident and respectful in Western societies, it may be construed as disrespectful or aggressive in certain East Asian societies. Similarly, the slapping of one's hand against the palm of the other hand is a common greeting amongst the Yoruba tribe of Nigeria, but in other societies, a simple nod suffices.

6.2. Rituals: The Threads Connecting Past to Present

Rituals act as the threads that seamlessly connect the fabric of time, linking individuals of the present generation to their historical past. They are enacted sequences of actions, filled with symbolic meaning, providing individuals a sense of identity and continuity.

Let's embark on a journey around the world, exploring different rituals that have shaped cultures. In Bali, locals engage in a ceremony called Melasti, a purification ritual to welcome the Balinese New Year where they clean themselves at a water source believed to hold purifying properties. On the other side of the globe, Native Americans hold a Pow Wow – a gathering to celebrate community, connection, dance, and heritage.

Rituals can also revolve around critical life events, from birth to maturation to marriage to mortality. The complex rites of passage in Bantu societies in Africa, the Bar and Bat Mitzvah in Jewish tradition, the elaborate wedding ceremonies of India, or the funeral pyres of Nepal, all reflect the diverse ways cultures commemorate these life-altering instances.

6.3. The Dynamic Nature of Etiquette and Rituals

Etiquette and rituals are not static entities. They metamorphose over time, adapting to the shifting currents of societal change while trying to maintain a bond with the historical past. Influences of global events, technological advancement, changing political ideologies, and increasing cross-cultural interaction continually shape and reshape these cultural practices. Such an example is the incorporation of digital etiquette – 'netiquette – in these modern times typified by increased virtual interaction.

6.4. Decoding the Unspoken Language

The decoding of this unspoken language of etiquette and rituals, while immensely complex, provides unprecedented insights into the communal psyche. It is akin to unlocking an elaborate cipher, where the clues lie embedded within the practices, waiting to be discovered and understood.

Studying social etiquette and rituals allows us to become culturally competent, moving beyond mere tolerance to a deeper understanding and appreciation of global diversity. While some norms may seem perplexing or even contradictory, understanding the context behind these practices reveal invaluable insights into the collective human endeavor.

All in all, the exploration of social etiquette and rituals opens up a world of understanding, diving deeply into the currents of cultural consciousness. They reflect a society's DNA, indicating its evolution, thoughts, perspectives, and values. As we navigate through this assembly of unique customs, we become part of a remarkable journey – a journey through time, history, and the very essence of what it means to be human. The examination of this unspoken language provides a mirror to the world, reflecting multiple vibrant cultures, each reflecting its unique essence into the grand human narrative. As we continue to decode this language, we learn more about each other and ourselves, fostering a sense of cross-cultural empathy and unity.

Chapter 7. Dances, Dramas, and Music: The Cultural Symphony

In the grand mosaic of culture, the tiles representing dances, dramas, and music shine with a glistening radiance, uniquely encapsulating the spirit of civilizations past and present. Harnessing the vibrancy of expressive body movements, the deep-set narratives of theatrical performances, and the lyrical harmonies of music, we embark on a symphonic journey into the cultural ethos of diverse societies.

7.1. Understanding Cultural Dance Forms

When cultures began to take shape across the globe, dance served as one of the chief communicative mediums, reflecting the identities, traditions, and histories of societies. The indigenous dance forms of Native Americans abstractly painted pictures of tribal legends and communal sentiments. Cautiously, we peel back the fascinating layers of the Maori dance, the Haka, resonating fiercely with symbolism and tribal pride of New Zealand's indigenous inhabitants.

From the graceful flamboyance of Spanish Flamenco, evoking fiery emotions encapsulated within dancer's pulsating movements, to the celestial grandeur of Indian classical dance Bharatanatyam or the rhythmic incantations of Africa's Djembe drums, every dance style encompasses a unique narrative. In-depth inquiry of these rhythmic art forms simultaneously immerses us in layers of cultural significance and metamorphosed traditions over centuries.

7.2. Journey through Cultural Drama

Next, we steer our exploration towards drama, a dynamic crucible of expression used ceremoniously and recreationally across diverse cultures. The ancient Greeks left an indelible imprint on world culture with their Tragedy and Comedy plays, where masked performers enacted stories of gods and men engaging in a symbolic narrative of victories, failures, and moral confrontations. These dramatic performances are mirrored in the elaborate Kathakali of Kerala, India, where performers transform into mythological entities vis-à-vis vibrant make-up, ornate costumes, and intense expression techniques.

In Japanese Noʘ drama, Zen Buddhism converges with Shinto rituals, birthing a distinctive theatrical form oscillating between our tangible world and the spiritual realm. From the passionate dramas of Shakespeare in Elizabethan England to the shadow puppetry of Indonesia's Wayang Kulit, cultural drama continues to project societal beliefs, reflections, and dreams.

7.3. Immerse in Cultural Music

There is no cultural exploration complete without venturing into the realm of music. Let's delve into how cultures across time and space have used music as an intimate expression tool - coupling lyrical prowess with musical genius, and effecting deep emotional resonance.

The lamenting blues of African Americans in the pre-civil rights era sung tales of societal struggle, segregation, and longing for freedom. Meanwhile, the pulsating beats of Samba music became synonymous with the Carnival of Brazil, reflecting the country's colonial history, diversity, and zest for life.

The serene strums of the Spanish guitar in Flamenco music serenade us while we contemplate the depths of sorrow and joy expressed in traditional Arabic Maqam music. Chinese classical music, based on pentatonic scale, takes us on a different audiovisual journey, with each twang of pipa telling a tale of ancient kingdoms and cherished folklore.

7.4. In Conclusion

Our journey concludes, leaving us marinating in a symphony of cultural understanding that has traversed the globe. The intricate connection between dance, drama, and music, and their inextricable relation to culture provide us a holistic insight into the philosophy, beliefs, and customs of societies. Understanding these art forms duly graduates us from being mere spectators into informed observers, capable of deciphering the subliminal messages within artistic expressions and thus realizing the essence of universal humanity in these cultural symphonies.

Chapter 8. Culinary Creations: A Taste of Tradition

As we embark on a delectable odyssey into the realm of gastronomic traditions and its eminently pivotal role in cultural narratives, it becomes vital to cast our net wide. We travel back to the roots of culinary creations, ferreting out the very essence of what drives these traditions, bringing them to life on a canvas as vivid as spices on a palette.

8.1. Culinary Basics: Understanding Food and Culture

Culinary traditions are a profound reflection of a culture's history, geography, and sociology. To begin to comprehend the depth and range of such traditions, it's prime that we consider the basic constituents of a community's diet. Food availability is dictated by geography and climate, both capricious and unwavering, shaping palates much before cultural nuances dibble their influence onto them. The abundance or scarcity of a particular grain, vegetable, or meat, in a region, often determined the base of many local delicacies conceived in the cauldrons of creativity and survival.

The interchange between communities, expedited by migration, trade, and conquest further diversified culinary landscapes, cumulating a symphony of flavors across cultures. Staple food adopted from foreign lands, spices sailed across the sprawling seas, and techniques shaped by alien tools all lent a helping hand in garnishing the platter of culinary tradition.

8.2. The Ingredients of Tradition: Building Blocks of Culinary Culture

Culinary traditions are enshrined in the emblematic elements of a culture's ingredients and cooking techniques. A solitary ingredient or a method of food preparation could embody centuries of history.

For instance, the use of olive oil is a distinctive feature in Mediterranean cuisine, influenced greatly by the region's climate, fertile for olive cultivation. Concurrently, the art of sushi preparation, deeply rooted in Japanese culture, is tied to the nation's geographical access to a wide variety of seafood.

In an enchanting ballet of molecules, the cooking techniques used can shape a culture's culinary identity as well. For example, the tandoori cooking style, largely identified with Indian and Middle Eastern cultures, requires a unique clay oven (tandoor) and specific marination techniques to achieve that smoky, charred flavor.

8.3. The Ceremonial Table: Food as Ritual

Food is not merely a sustenance provider—it's sometimes, the pulsating heartbeat of a culture's social and religious fabric. Whether it's a sacrificial offering on a temple's altar or a laden table at a Thanksgiving dinner, food forms the epicenter of ceremonies, around which social interactions whirl.

The sanctity associated with certain foods transcends into dietary laws and restrictions across cultures. Hindu traditions, for instance, prohibit the consumption of beef, while Islamic and Jewish laws dictate specific methods of animal slaughter for meat to be considered 'halal' or 'kosher.'

8.4. The Gourmet Tapestry: Regional Specialties and Signature Dishes

Peppered across the globe are an array of signature dishes, signifying the culinary essence of a region. Whether it's the hearty cassoulet stew savored in the South of France, or the tangy Chaat enjoyed on the bustling streets of India, or the wholesome Borscht soup relished in Ukrainian homes, these signature recipes are the ambassadors representing their culture on the global culinary stage.

These regional specialties are so deeply intertwined with a culture's identity that they become family heirlooms, passed down through generations, their tastes, fragrances, and techniques cherished and preserved as carefully as a precious artifact.

8.5. Culinary Diplomacy: Food as an Ambassador

Food, the universal language of flavor, acts as a bridge, connecting cultures across geographical boundaries. As we swap recipes and share meals, we gradually soften the sharp edges of misunderstanding that often cloud our perception of foreign cultures.

With humble beginnings in local kitchens, the culinary traditions have traversed onto the global stage, bringing communities together, in the spirit of understanding and admiration, through their idiosyncratic gastronomic narratives.

Culinary traditions are far more than mere gustatory indulgence. They are a rich, complex blend of history, geography, religion, and cultural values, as intrinsic to a culture's identity as its language or art forms. Digesting the ethos behind the 'Culinary Creations: A Taste of Tradition', serves to sate more than hunger—it feeds the insatiable curiosity about the world's beautiful and diverse cultures.

Chapter 9. Threads of Belief: Religion and Spirituality

Embarking on this enlightening exploration into the realm of religious belief and spirituality, it is important to underscore the integral role of such traditions in adding depth and diversity to human cultures the world over. Whether manifested in the mystical expressions of spirituality, or the structured principles of organized religion, we discern an essential thread that connects humanity's past, present, and future.

9.1. Understanding the Basis of Belief

The first point of departure on our voyage is deep within the human psyche: the psychological foundations of faith. Religion and spirituality, irrespective of the number of forms they assume, are situated in the human need to comprehend the world. Humans seek to interpret and deal with phenomena that lie beyond their immediate understanding, often through the lens of faith. It is through these systems of belief that societies not only explain their origin from an ethereal perspective, but also develop shared values, catapulting their security, harmony, and communal engagement.

9.2. The Evolution of Religious Practices

While the origin of religious practices remains an enigma shrouded in the veils of prehistory, the subsequent evolution is well-documented. Emerging from animistic beliefs of primal societies, we've observed an expansion into increasingly organized, complex systems, mirroring societal developments. From the pantheon of deities in polytheistic religions to monotheistic faith traditions, there lies an undeniable dynamism in religion's transcultural development. One must also consider the advent and cosmic significance of atheism and agnosticism as evidence of parallel evolutions challenging established religious norms.

9.3. The Lingua Franca of Faith: Sacred Texts and Symbols

These complex systems of belief hinge on sacred texts and symbols, which serve as a lingua franca across faith communities. Sacred texts, be they the Bible, The Quran, Vedas, Torah, or any other, are repositories of religious wisdom, doctrine, and teachings. Crucial for maintaining continuity, they deliver the seeds of faith into every epoch, permitting an individual to readily access divine instructions. Symbols, on the other hand, provide a form of visual language, communicating the epitome of the belief structure.

9.4. Culture and Ceremonies: The Power of Ritual

Human spirituality often manifests in a culture's rituals and ceremonies. Embedded within every ritual, from the Christian Eucharist to Hindu Diwali, there's a fundamental necessity for communion and the affirmation of shared faith. The potency of these rituals is evident in their ability to connect generations, creating a continuum of shared beliefs. Moreover, they serve as direct encounters with the divine, fostering spiritual growth and community cohesion.

9.5. Sacred Spaces: Temples, Churches, and Mosques

Tangible extensions of faith manifest in sacred spaces, serving both as physical embodiments of spiritual ideals and vibrant cultural landmarks. From the Gothic cathedrals in the West to the serene Buddhist temples of the East, each structure reflects its faith's unique cosmology. Additionally, these architectural marvels function as communal spaces that facilitate shared experiences and encourage social bonds.

9.6. Faith and Social Dynamics

Faith shapes societies and their norms. The interplay between belief systems and societal norms steers moral compasses, dictating definitions of right and wrong. The spiritual realities of worldviews continually shape and are shaped by political, economic, and societal domains, illustrating the dynamic relationship between religion and society.

9.7. The Future of Faith: Syncretism and Secularization

As we approach the future of belief systems, we witness two divergent trends: syncretism and secularization. Syncretism refers to the blending of religious traditions, resulting in interfaith harmonization. In contrast, secularization characterizes societies turning away from religious practice towards more secular life perspectives. Both trends outline the astounding adaptability of belief in an ever-changing society.

In conclusion, our exploration shows us that the innumerable threads of belief contribute to the grand tapestry of global culture, painting a vibrant picture infused with diverse religious and spiritual practices. These threads of belief weave the path towards a deeper intercultural understanding, encouraging us to appreciate the rich diversity prevalent amongst us. Through the lens of religion and spirituality, we gather glimpses of humanity's quest for purpose, unity, and transcendence, woven through the ages and continuing to evolve. To grasp these threads is to begin understanding the complex and wondrous worlds within our world.

And so, we embark on our journey towards the next captivating arena: 'Sacred Spaces: Architecture and Sacred Sites,' where we will delve into the world of extraordinary physical manifestations of belief.

Chapter 10. Sacred Spaces: Architecture and Sacred Sites

The journey to understanding other cultures often begins with an exploration of the physical structures they choose to erect as a reflection of their complex beliefs and value systems. Architecture, in its myriad forms, is the most palpable manifestation of cultural identity, telling the long, winding stories of civilizations often more precisely than the written word. Nowhere is this more apparent than in the sacred spaces that societies build.

10.1. The Universal Language of Sacred Spaces

At the simplest level, sacred spaces are a universal phenomenon - a common thread present in all cultures, throughout history, tying our collective human narrative together. Though diverse in structure and design, these spaces tend to serve similar purposes - as realms for worship, quiet contemplation, and the celebration of important cultural events. They can range from towering edifices of grandeur to humbling open-air spaces set against the backdrop of nature.

Brilliantly, the sanctity of these architectural marvels transcends the borders that separate us, exuding an inherent respect that humbles even the indifferent. This, underlined by the zeal and reverence that inspired their creation and the hopes, dreams, and fears that continue to fuel their preservation, makes them more than just structures; they are living, breathing dwellings of humanity's rich spiritual history.

10.2. Religious Architecture: A Kaleidoscope of Faith

Religious architecture is the most apparent form of sacred spaces, with designs that reflect the core beliefs and sentiments of respective faiths. Examine the disciplined geometry of Islamic mosques, for instance. Intricate Arabesque, labyrinthine ceilings hint towards an expression of the faith's reverence for order, unity, and the infinite nature of God.

Contrast this with the Gothic cathedrals of Christianity, with their foreboding spires striving for the heavens, their resplendent stained-glass windows narrating biblical tales infused with profound moral lessons.

Take a trip to Buddhism's heartlands, and the muted minimalism of the architectural designs preaches the principles of austerity and detachment, while the towering Stupas symbolize the path to enlightenment.

Hindu temples, on the other hand, narrate tales of mythical grandeur and divine power through their elaborate carvings and detailed symbolism, speaking volumes about the faith's polytheistic nature and its pantheon of deities.

10.3. Vernacular Sacred Spaces: A Manifestation of Local Identities

Religious structures are not the only examples of sacred spaces. Local communities build vernacular sacred spaces – structures that merge the divine and the day-to-day. These include sacred wells, groves, indigenous burial sites, and even dwellings. Each of these examples reflects a deep spiritual connection with nature, ancestor worship, and communal identity.

These spaces blur the line between the mundane and the divine, serving as daily reminders of the community's spiritual beliefs and offerings a space where individuals can connect with forces beyond their immediate physical reality.

10.4. The Bridge between Yesterday and Today

The idea of sacred spaces entails more than just religious intent. It encompasses the collective memory of a community or a civilization. Architecture embodies each civilization's ethos, the genius of its builders, the social norms that governed its creation, and the technological breakthroughs that made it possible. It serves as an unchangeable touchstone, preserving the past even as the present moves forward relentlessly. It's vital, then, to comprehend these spaces not just in terms of their physical form, but also by the continuum of time they represent.

In studying these spaces, we unravel the wisdom of ancients, gleaning invaluable insights into their ways of perceiving the world.

10.5. The Future: A Marriage of Tradition and Innovation

As we venture further into the 21st Century, the concept of sacred spaces is rapidly evolving. While maintaining a respectful deference to traditional sacred sites, societies are also exploring the spiritual capacity of non-traditional spaces that transcend any one religious faith.

Spaces for meditation, yoga, or even public parks that emphasize harmony with nature are becoming the 'new' sacred spaces in our societies. They are places where individuals and communities come together to reflect, rejuvenate, and seek solace.

As we progress, the novel interplay between traditional and contemporary interpretations of sacred spaces will further challenge and shape the architectural landscape, generating profound opportunities for spiritual exploration and cultural dialogue.

10.6. Conclusion

It is vital, then, in our journey towards understanding and appreciating diverse cultures, to delve deep into the architecture of their sacred spaces. It is here, in this realm of the human spirit, that the barriers of time and geography are stripped down, fostering a shared response of reverence and respectful wonder.

After journeying through the philosophical and architectural perspectives of sacred spaces, one thing remains clear: these spaces are much more than their physical constituents. They are spiritual embodiments showcasing the human pursuit of meaning and connection to the universe.

Whether you find profound spiritual significance within these spaces, marvel at their architectural ingenuity, or recognize them as invaluable cultural treasures, they undeniably hold a powerful sway over our collective human psyche, binding together the threads of our diverse identities into a shared tapestry of human experience.

Chapter 11. Celebrating Diversity: Key Insights and Future Perspectives

In an epoch marked by rapid globalization and technological advancements, the need for cross-cultural understanding has never been more essential. As we endeavor to comprehend the intricate web weaved by the threads of diversity, we will embark on a journey that navigates the vibrant plethora of cultures across the globe. Each one brimming with distinctive practices, beliefs, traditions, and histories, which ultimately culminate into a rich tapestry of human experience.

11.1. Understanding Cultural Diversity

Cultural diversity refers to the variety of human societies or cultures within a specific region, or around the world as a whole. Varied perspectives on life, stemming from varying cultural backgrounds, enrich humanity and propel us towards greater intellectual exchanges and mutual growth. It isn't merely about acknowledging these differences but understanding and cherishing them wholeheartedly.

Each culture is like a unique, intricate art piece. It carefully exhibits the values, norms, symbols, material culture, and language embodying the spirit of its people. These distinctions shape their perceptions, logic systems, and attitudes towards various aspects of life, such as relationship dynamics, societal structure, and even view of the natural world.

11.2. The Role of Globalization

In the current era of globalization, the world is not merely a vast, diversified space; it's interconnected and interdependent, virtually shrunk into a "global village". These close interactions inevitably lead to an exchange of cultural norms, ideas, and practices. However, such an exchange can also expose stark contrasts and conflicts among cultures.

Hence, the need for cultural sensitivity – the ability to respect, appreciate and understand these differences, becomes essential. It helps bridge the gaps, manage conflicts, and contributes to smoother interpersonal interactions. The exchange doesn't solely imply influencing each other but more about learning, understanding, and growing together, strengthening the global fabric of humanity.

11.3. Cultural Relativism and Ethnocentrism

The concept of cultural relativism argues that all cultures, irrespective of their unconventional practices, possess intrinsic worth and merit understanding rather than judgement. Simply put, each culture has its own valid worldview, scaled according to its unique historical context, environmental constraints, and lifestyle needs.

Contrarily, ethnocentrism often fosters cultural prejudice and biases. It insinuates superiority of one's native culture, promoting a lens view that inadvertently affects their understanding of different cultures. As we continue celebrating cultural diversity, it's essential to shun ethnocentric attitudes and adopt a more broad-minded, inclusive perspective.

11.4. Celebrating Diversity: Fountainhead of Creativity and Innovation

Diversity is an inexhaustible source of inspiration, creativity and innovation. In the field of arts, literature, music, or even sciences and technology, exposure to differing cultural nuances has routinely spurred unique perspectives and groundbreaking ideas. Diversity enables exchange, which in turn emanates innovation.

Moreover, cultural diversity enhances social development by broadening individuals' horizons, teaching acceptance and empathy. It allows us to see past our limited perspective, promotes mutual respect, and conjures social bonds that bind societies together in harmony.

11.5. Navigating through Multiculturalism and Inclusion

Multiculturalism supports the co-existence of diverse cultures, promoting mutual respect and equality among them. It promises a society where one can maintain their cultural identity without fear of being marginalized.

Inclusion goes hand-in-hand with multiculturalism as it ensures individuals or groups are not excluded on the grounds of their culture. By fostering an inclusive environment, we embolden individuals to share their unique perspectives, contributing to the vibrant diversity.

As we unravel this last chapter, we hope it provides food for thought for deep-diving into the world of cultural diversity. It's not merely about tolerating differences, but accepting and celebrating them.

Only by doing so can we foster a world that thrives on mutual respect, equality, and shared understanding, diminishing the barriers that divide us and cherishing the myriad hues that the human tapestry brings.

Remember, "Diversity is the one true thing we all have in common. Celebrate it every day." Here's saying goodbye, with the hope that you continue to wander in the labyrinth of global cultures, discovering, learning and celebrating the wealth of diversity that it offers. This is where our guide ends, but the journey of understanding and appreciating cultural diversity continues.